TO PERSONAL ACCOUNTABILITY

INCORPORATING SELF RESPONSIBILITY, CHARACTER AND INTEGRITY INTO YOUR LIFE

MOE RUSSELL

outskirts
press

Take the High Road to Personal Accountability: Incorporating
Self Responsibility, Character and Integrity into your Life
All Rights Reserved
Copyright © 2021 Moe Russell
v2.0

Outskirts Press, Inc.
http://www.outskirtspress.com

ISBN: 978-1-9772-4272-3

Outskirts Press and the "OP" logo are trademarks belonging to
Outskirts Press, Inc.

PRINTED IN THE UNITED STATES OF AMERICA

TABLE OF CONTENTS

PREFACE

I was born and raised on a farm and have spent my entire career either in agricultural finance or as President of Russell Consulting Group. That is an organization that I cofounded with my partner Terry Jones in 1998 to provide financial and commodity marketing advice to farmers and ranchers. The genesis of this book came from what I have learned working with some of the finest people in the world: those who grow things and care for animals. The first lesson in taking the high road came from my father while I was in my early teens. I will share that story later.

Some of what I will share is my experiences in taking the high road, and some were where I did not take it but could have and should have. I do firmly believe that once we make a commitment to take the higher road to personal accountability, it becomes second nature and is a part of our subconscious mind—the part of our mind that takes over when we are too scared, or too tired, or too busy to consciously think about our actions.

Chapter One

———⁂———

THE CHANCE FOR
A BETTER WORLD

ONE OF MY heroes is Peter F. Drucker, a long-time teacher, author, and management consultant whose writings and teachings set many of the philosophical and practical basics of decision making. Drucker, who was born in Austria, shares a story in his book *The Adventures of a Bystander*, where as a young boy he was watching the Austrian Army march down his street. He was contemplating joining the Austrian Army, but suddenly he realized that his life contribution would not be in doing but by consulting, so he spent much of his career being a bystander, and he contributed much in that role.

We consultants make fun of our industry. It has been said, those that can, do; those who cannot, consult. Perhaps that is why I am not a full-time farmer. As my first mentor in Farm Credit told me, "I will never be useless; I can always be used as a horrible example!"

Farming is a business where anything can go wrong and it seems like it does. Too much rain, not enough rain, breakdowns, family disagreements, losing a rented farm, employees leaving, difficulty finding and keeping good help, untimely death, divorce—the list never seems to end.

I've heard others: "The bank doesn't understand our operation," "I want to expand, but I just can't find any land," "Others don't work as hard as I do. It's not fair. Some people have all the luck."

I believe that luck when used with the word *good* is a four-letter word people use to describe the successes of others, and when used with the word *bad* is a word they use to describe their own failures.

A very human tendency as a reaction to the problem is to have the attitude, "Who can I blame for my problem?" When the first two people on earth got in trouble, what happened? The man blamed the woman and the woman blamed the serpent!

Taking personal responsibility when things go wrong is tough, but having that attitude makes for quicker and better solutions. Life teaches us all in ways that hurt, but they are good lessons. We cannot control what other people do or say, or events occurring around us. The only thing we really have control over is ourselves and how we react to those events.

The most successful people are the ones who believe they control their own destiny and realize they are not being controlled by the weather, the government, the competition, or their neighbors. Those are, of course, factors that affect us all, but they should not be the ones that overwhelm us. Successful people recognize that events happen that are outside their control and plan for them.

And this is exactly why personal accountability is so important and why people and organizations that demonstrate accountability stand out.

In truth, there are reasons things go wrong. People make mistakes. The ball gets dropped. Stuff happens. Business and families can be complicated, confusing, and complex.

Any one of us on any given day could go on with reasons why things go wrong. However, if we play them back they often sound like excuses, and oftentimes that is all they really are.

It seems like the popular thing to do today is to blame someone else, whine, point fingers, play victim, become entitled, and expect others to bail us out of our bad choices.

I believe if we all took responsibility for our own actions, learned from them and moved forward (we all took the higher road to personal accountability), there would be less unemployment, fewer children with one parent caring for them, less government debt, less taxes, and greater wealth.

It's easy to take the high road to personal accountability when things are going great. It's tough when you get caught up in the vortex of everything going wrong. I've been in both of those positions both professionally and personally. The biggest challenge is dealing with the human emotion of fear.

Tom Kelly of the University of California, Berkeley, Haas School of Management gives clients strategies to get past the four fears that hold most people back from taking control of bad conditions. They are:

- Fear of the messy unknown
- Fear of being judged
- Fear of Taking the First Step
- Fear of losing Control

Breaking fear down into these four areas and thinking through what you need to do, how you will do it, and when you will do it, really helps. Simply saying "I like" or "I wish" rather than "That will never work" is a good strategy, Kelly adds.

Over a decade ago, my wife, Mardi, and I were at a conference where we met Jay Riffenbary and his wife and received a copy of Jay's book *No Excuse*. I have reread it several times. This fall I read it again as I felt myself falling into the habit of blaming others. I highly recommend reading it.

Jay, a West Point Academy graduate, says there are only four responses a lower-classman cadet can give to an upper classman. They are: "Yes, Sir"; "No, Sir"; "I don't understand, Sir"; and "No excuse, Sir."

Having the "No Excuse" attitude and mentality gets us out of the "why me" or the victimization attitude I see so prevalent in our families, our society, and our leaders.

When we form the habit of taking personal accountability by looking in the mirror and saying, "I think I see the problem," things start to get better, we move forward, and people like being around us. I always try to ask myself, "What is right?" rather than "Who is right?" I have noticed that when I answer that question and act on the answer, people around me begin to change their behavior.

Chapter Two

BAD DAYS HAPPEN

I AM BLESSED with a wonderful family. My wife Mardi and I have been married 46 years and have two children. Our daughter Tana is married to a wonderful man, Jamie, and she has an eight -year-old son, Jack, and a three year -old daughter, Dylan. They are the light of our lives. We have a son, Jared, in heaven. When he was 20 years old between his freshman and sophomore year at Iowa State University, he was working a summer job at Coulter Marine Lake Panorama, Iowa. We were living in Omaha at the time.

It was June of 1998 and Mardi and I were sitting on the patio at our home in Omaha having a cocktail, when all of a sudden Mardi started sobbing. I, not knowing anything was wrong, asked what the problem was. Mardi said, "Moe, I have the feeling something really bad is going to happen to Jared." I wrongly dismissed her concern. We knew Jared had a rough first year at college grade-wise, but he seemed fine. That was my best lesson in learning to listen to "women's intuition." Believe me it is real.

Two months later, on August 13th, we were awakened by the doorbell at about 3 AM, and standing at the front door was an officer with the Nebraska Highway Patrol. Mardi immediately began crying and said, "Something bad happened to Jared." The patrolman indicated Jared had been in a car accident. I said, "How is he?" The patrolman gave us a blank look that sent a chill down our spine. He said, "It is not good."

The patrolman said Jared had been flown by air ambulance to Methodist Hospital in Des Moines. We thanked the officer, got Tana up, and headed by car for the two-hour trip to Des Moines.

Shortly into the trip we considered taking a charter plane from Omaha, as I had done many times on business trips when I worked for Farm Credit. To see if that would be practical; we called Methodist hospital and talked to the emergency room nurse to see how Jared was. The nurse said he had already died. She broke protocol in conveying that message over the phone. It was the worst day of our lives.

Jared had been with a dozen or more of his friends that night and was driving too fast in a friend's car. Another friend, Jill, was with Jared. The accident occurred on P58 south of Perry, Iowa. Jared lost control of the car and it backed into a telephone pole at a very high rate of speed, shearing off the pole and killing Jared instantly. Jill crawled out the back window of the car and went to a nearby farmhouse for help.

When we arrived at the emergency room, all of Jared's friends he had been with that night were there. They looked like they had seen a ghost and were very sad. We all joined hands, surrounding Jared's body, and said the Lord's

Prayer. Then I looked at all of his friends and said, "Mardi and I want you all to know one thing. We do not blame any of you for what happened last night. We raised Jared to be accountable for his own actions and he took the rap for this one." Each one of those friends is now a lifelong friend of ours. I was in so much shock, my comments had to be on autopilot, but taking the higher road was definitely the right thing to do. Trying to place blame would have been totally counterproductive.

As J. Barry Griswold and Bob Jennings in their Book, *The Adversity Paradox* point out, in many cases adversity brings opportunity. With the adversity of Jared's death, the opportunity was we inherited Roscoe, a three-month-old yellow Lab. What a blessing. Roscoe offered comfort in our grief, laughter in our joy of raising him, and many years of true friendship. As you may know, raising a Labrador retriever from a pup has its challenges. A month after Jared's death I was in my basement office at home in Omaha and Roscoe was with me. I inadvertently dropped a blue-ink Bic pen off the front of my desk. Not seeing it happen, Roscoe picked up the pen and ran up to the white sofa in our living room and chewed it to bits! Blue ink all over a white sofa! All we could do was laugh.

Chapter Three

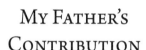

MY FATHER'S
CONTRIBUTION

BEING RAISED ON a farm was a blessing. I have five brothers and no sisters. We had much fun, a lot of hard work, and faith, community, and friends that molded our character. I would not be what I am today if not for that experience.

My father, Richard Russell, was born and raised on a farm near Mt. Vernon, Iowa. He and his brother farmed the family farm together beginning when he was in his twenties. At that time the government would not draft two brothers from the same farm. When WWII came he and his brother made an agreement that whoever was drafted would go and the other would stay home and farm the home place. My uncle was drafted and, after the war, decided to make the Army his career. At that point my dad decided to set out on his own and buy his own farm. He had been very successful feeding cattle on a rented farm until the fall of 1955, when he decided to purchase his own farm. He purchased 320 acres near Monticello, Iowa.

At the time of that purchase, he was in sound financial shape. Between the fall of 1955 and March of 1956 when he closed on the farms, the cattle market crashed and he did not even have the down payment for the farm. He had to borrow that from the bank. Our family spent the next ten years just getting by. I remember we only had ice cream once a week, on Friday night. We were probably considered poor during those years but we loved life and didn't feel poor at all.

My father taught me that God should be the center of my life. We went to Mass every Sunday. One Easter the weather was awful and the roads were so bad my father and brother went to Mass on a tractor. He went to weekend retreats with the Catholic Church. Many nights, I recall heading to bed after studying, and observing him kneeling by his bed praying.

When we moved to the new farm, the farmhouse on the farm my parents bought did not have running water, inside toilets, or central heating. I was in first grade and had to move from my school to a Catholic school. There were two grades in the same room. It was very difficult for me.

On the farm, many times we would trade equipment and labor with neighbors. On one occasion a neighbor asked to borrow a hay rack. That is a wagon with a wooden flat bed, back ledge about four to six feet high to hold hay bales, and all three other sides open.

My father willingly loaned him the wagon. While using it, the neighbor fell through the board on the front end of the wagon and wrenched his knee, which required surgery. As a result of the neighbor's injury, he sued my father for negligence because he claimed my father knew or should have known the board on the wagon was faulty. The suit was for $25,000. We were devastated. First of all a community like ours was so closely knit, most issues like this were worked out. In the 1960s $25,000 was the equivalent of $130,000 to $150,000 today. We all went to the same church and we were ashamed that we were being sued by a neighbor.

We of course had insurance that would have covered most of the claim, but that was not the point. The neighbor came to my father and indicated that he would like us to admit negligence, saying that he knew the insurance company would pay the claim and we could all live happily thereafter. Luckily my father took the high road and said, "I did not know the wagon was faulty, if I had I would not have loaned it to you. No deal."

The case went to trial and my family was found not guilty.

This was my first lesson in taking the high road. Had my father compromised his principles we would still have had great friends, good times, and a happy community; however, we would not have done the right thing.

This had a powerful impact on my development. As Peter Drucker has said, "Character and Integrity by itself accomplishes nothing, but its absence faults everything."

Living on the farm was hard work, but very rewarding. We would get up at 5:30 AM to help care for animals. My job was to help my mother, Mary, milk a herd of registered Jerseys. My father cared for the pigs and other cattle and my other brothers helped him.

One learning experience I had was trying to milk a young cow that had never had a mechanical milk machine obtain her milk. She was frightened and kicked the entire milk machine off and it ended up in the gutter. I proceeded to yell at her and slap her. Unknown to me, my father happened to be walking by the milking barn and heard the commotion. What he said I will never forget. He said, "Maurice, every cow in this barn is a lady; I want you to treat them like one."

This was a good lesson on mercy, animal welfare, and taking the higher road.

After morning chores we would get cleaned up, eat breakfast, and be ready for the school bus at 7:30 AM. We were nearly 10 miles from school, so we were one of the first on the bus and it was about an hour ride to and from school. I envied kids who lived within walking distance of school.

Growing up on a diversified grain and livestock farm was a neat experience. Experiencing the changes of seasons was neat. In the spring the snow and ice would melt, giving way to new life and green pastures. Probably the most satisfying was watching new life start and grow in the baby pigs and baby calves.

We had a lot of fun also; with having five brothers around, there was never a dull moment. We laughed a lot, fought a lot, and learned a lot. I remember my two older brothers in a fight where one chased the other into the cornfield with a rock and screamed, "If you ever come out of there, I will kill you!!" I am sure he didn't really mean it when things calmed down.

The greatest lesson I learned was "What you sow is what you reap." Life has consequences; there are cause-and-effect relationships, and although many things are beyond one's control, such as weather, insects, and so on, hard work will pay off.

Although our family did not have much money, we ate well and I never went hungry. We had all the meat, milk, and eggs we needed, as they were grown on the farm. After recently reading the book *We Were the Lucky Ones* by Georgia Hunter, which is a book about a Jewish family in Poland during WWII, I realized how fortunate we were to be born and raised on a farm, and having never been real hungry.

Chapter Four

---ᴀᴀᴀ---

MARDI

MY WIFE MARDENE Russell is the love of my life and the best example of one who has spent her entire life taking the higher road. She is from a small town in Iowa and her father was in WWII, and then was the postmaster in that town. They, too, did not have much money and none of her siblings went to college. Mardi wanted to be a nurse, but her parents discouraged that. They said, "Why don't you just get a job?" She took the higher road and went to nurse's training, paid her own tuition and living, and a year later graduated as an LPN.

After we were married, she went back to school and earned a Medical Assistant degree while we lived in Omaha, Nebraska.

My Farm Credit career required us to move four times to different states, and Mardi had to quit her job each time and she never complained, even though she had good jobs and a good career. She went out of her way to take the higher road.

She was very good at raising our family. During 5th grade, our son Jared was falling behind in school. The school said they thought he had Attention Deficit Disorder (ADD). Mardi and I said, "Why do you say that?" They said he had manual dexterity problems as well as concentration problems. The school wanted to put Jared in a special needs class which would not be acceptable to us. We said Jared at age 10–11 is an accomplished drummer; he could play "Wipeout" without a problem, so manual dexterity was not a problem. Also we said, "He can play with his Legos, building elaborate things for hours—he does not have a concentration problem."

The bottom line is Mardi said "no way are we going to have Jared in a special education program, let us work with him."

My time to work with Jared was limited as I was in the worst of the Farm Crisis. Luckily we made it through it.

Mardi spent hours every day working with Jared to be a better student. She achieved that: he was advanced to the next grade and excelled in junior high and high school.

The lesson I learned from Mardi is, "Don't give up on anyone, help them any way you can and they will succeed." Jared did and what a tribute to Mardi for taking the higher and often tougher road to personal accountability.

Mardi has two professional nursing degrees, LPN and Medical Assistant, but changed her career in 1995. She began working for an interior home-decorating business. She enjoyed it so much that for the last 21 years she has owned her own decorating business, Interiors by Mardi.

Chapter Five

The Military

I WAS THE only one of the six Russell boys to serve in the military. I was in college in 1969 and my draft status was 1D. That meant I was at the top of the list for being drafted as soon as I graduated in 1971. This was at the peak of the Vietnam War. I preferred not to go to Vietnam, so I joined the Iowa Army National Guard. You have to decide for yourself whether or not I took the high road at that time.

I will say this: a year later the lottery was

established and my number was 306! I would never have been drafted.

Whatever you might feel about the war, I have never regretted my decision. It was a great experience. I spent six months of active duty in Fort Gordon, Georgia. I spent two weeks a summer on military duty and a weekend a month on duty. It helped me with my college expenses. I made about $100 a month from the Guard, and with my income from washing dishes at our fraternity it provided most of my spending money.

I learned much from the experience. The military has the best management, tactical, operational, and human resource training in the world, and I was extremely thankful to be able to take advantage of it.

In the six years of my original commitment I started basic training as an E-1 the lowest enlisted rank and ended as acting First Sergeant.

Chapter Six

———— ᨆᨆ ————

THE CZECH EXPERIENCE

IN 1992 I had the great opportunity presented to me by the state of Iowa to do a consulting project in Eastern Europe. It was far before I started my consulting business. I spent time in Hungary and the Czech Republic.

Most people I talk to in my seminars cannot tell me when the Berlin Wall fell. It was November 9, 1989. This is a very important date.

In our consulting project, I worked with a remarkable man, Delbert Heisterkamp from Onawa, Iowa.

One day after our work we stopped at a pub in Prague 1 to have a pint of beer. It was about 5 PM.

We met a gentleman who was a gynecologist in Prague. He was 42 years old. His age is important to my story, as he was born after the Communists took control of the Czech Republic. After a short conversation, it became apparent to us that he had been there a long while before us.

In a conversation with him we asked what his salary was. He said $400 a month U.S. I replied, "That is interesting, what does a cab driver make in Prague?" He responded, "$400 per month U.S."

I recall asking the doctor why he was a doctor and not a cab driver. He said they tested them at an early age and that determined what they would do.

Later on in our consulting project we met another person in Prague. He was an administrator in a drug rehabilitation center in Prague. However, he was born and raised on a dairy farm about 75 kilometers north of Prague. When he was 12 years old the Communists came and took over their dairy farm. I asked him what they left them and he took his keys and change out of his pockets, and he said, "They even took this."

In the three years after the fall of the Berlin Wall, he had already acquired the deed back to his family farm, he had retrofitted the dairy parlor, he already purchased a herd of purebred Guernsey bred heifers, and he was going about an objective of reestablishing that dairy farm like a "heat-seeking missile."

He is an Entrepreneur. It is humbling to appreciate that he probably lay awake at night for 44 years thinking about what he would do if he ever had the opportunity to get the family farm back.

That doctor we met in the pub did not have a clue what it was to be an Entrepreneur. It was because he was born into the Communist system. He did not know any better. He could not define entrepreneurship for us.

This experience taught me to appreciate my being allowed to choose my life work and to do it in a free-enterprise system, and have the freedom to take the higher road to personal accountability.

Chapter Seven

GOALS

I HAVE ALWAYS had written goals. The reason I do is that at an early age I read about a Yale University study where the researchers interviewed the 1951 graduating class of Yale University. They had a series of questions, but they were mainly concentrated around whether the graduates had written goals. Only 4% had written goals.

Twenty years later in 1971 the researchers interviewed the surviving members of that 1951 class, and the 4% that had written goals had accumulated more wealth than the other 96% combined.

One of my goals was written in 1976. I wanted to have an MBA by the time I was 50 years old. When I was 48 years old living in Omaha, Nebraska, I learned about a two year Executive MBA program at University of Nebraska at Omaha. So I did the math and enrolled in the program. It was one of the greatest experiences of my life. In fact, it was the genesis for me starting my own business. Of the class of 30 about a third were from large companies like AT&T, a third from smaller businesses, and a third were entrepreneurs. That experience motivated me to become an Entrepreneur.

I had a goal of starting my own business. I went to one of my customers, Terry Jones, and asked him if he thought there would be an opportunity of providing financial and commodity marketing services to farmers and ranchers. He agreed there was an opportunity. So we each put $1,000 cash in the business and started providing our service. We have been richly blessed. Our original goal was to have 100 clients in three years, and we had 100 clients in 9 months and 17 days. It was a great business with a great cash flow for 18 years. We have since sold the company to CHS (Cenex Harvest States), the largest farmer-owned cooperative in America. They provide grain handling and processing, risk management, and fuel refining to farmers and ranchers. I do not miss corporate America at all. Taking the high road has worked much better. Terry has been the greatest partner in the world. I have so much respect for him.

I had a great career with Farm Credit for 26 years, starting as a loan officer, and when I left I was in charge of their 83 lending offices in Iowa, Nebraska, South Dakota, and Wyoming. My career ended abruptly and I did not know why and did not ask. Taking the high road on my way home that day has proven very rewarding.

Four years later I received a call from a former employee. He said he was the reason I left Farm Credit. He said I'd passed him up for a promotion, and he vowed to end my career for doing that. I thanked him. Several years later he died of cancer. I went to his memorial service.

AFTERWORD
By Richard Wymore

WHERE I COME INTO THE STORY

I first met Moe when he came to work at the Farm Credit Bank of Omaha where I had been employed for two or three years. Moe was part of the second class of trainees that were hired by the Farm Credit Bank to be soon hired by one of the Production Credit Associations (PCAs) in our four-state area. I was the youngest man on staff and the only single one and so it fell upon me to be the tour guide to the wonders of Omaha, Nebraska, for the members of that class. Most of those wonders took place after 5 PM, and so we spent most of our early evenings discovering life in the big city and life in general.

I remember one of my first impressions of Moe was that he seemed to have a strong sense of himself. He was very outgoing, treated everyone the same, and yet seemed to find himself as the leader of most of the groups he became part of. I have since come to realize that the reason for his success was not just that he was smart—although he was—or that he had a great personality—which he did. It was that he treated everyone exactly the same.

I also became aware very soon that Moe would be willing to stay up and talk as long as the beer kept flowing and someone stayed to talk with him, and he accepted personal responsibility for his apparent inability to recognize his need to end the discussion and go to bed. But he never lost a step the next morning. He was at work, ready to go and looking good and full of questions.

Within a month or so, he was hired by the PCA back in eastern Iowa where he had grown up and soon had moved into a large house in

DeWitt, Iowa, with two other PCA employees. This house, known as the White House, was legend in DeWitt as the place for fun and conversation.

In a couple of years, Moe was married and back in Omaha in a credit job with FCB and we were able to include our wives in our friendship. Our favorite couple's night out in Omaha was to go to the Firehouse Dinner Theatre. We decided who was going to pay for the tickets including the meal based on the winner of the Nebraska–Iowa State football game. As a native Nebraskan and a rabid Cornhusker fan, I was always willing to give Moe way more points than I should have. And I won nearly every year anyway. But, since this evening was a pretty expensive night for one couple to stand, we agreed that the loser would buy the meals and the winner would buy the drinks. As the perennial winner, my bill at the end of the night was regularly larger than Moe's.

I did not grow up on a farm, but I soon learned how important relationships were to the young men like Moe who came to work for FCB in the big city. They were immediately accepted as

part of the Farm Credit Family. We worked together all week, and many Friday nights we got
together with our wives at someone's house and
talked about the week, our families, and our
values. I have worked for several organizations
in my life, but this group of farmers is the only
organization where I am still, 35 years later,
close friends with them all. We were, and still
are, a family. We worked hard and we played
hard and we cared about each other. Still do.

Moe kept moving up the ladder and soon was
on to Mitchell, South Dakota, where he was
key man in the supervisor of the South Dakota
and Wyoming PCAs. It was during this time
that Moe and I had one of our most meaning-
ful conversations. We had all been involved in
upgrading the salary program for the system
and had spent quite a lot of time develop-
ing job descriptions for ourselves and others.
As a result of this, Moe decided that he and I
should both develop Life Descriptions, and we
had several long conversations about what was
really important in our lives and what success
would look like. I still have my life description
and refer to it occasionally. At my last review I
gave myself a pretty good grade but still have

some areas to work on. I have not changed a word of the life description since the day I wrote it. I am most proud of item #6 on mine:

"To never worry about yesterday, to live each today to the fullest, and to plan for tomorrow without fear." I still have Moe's as well. Here is my favorite from his: "Promote and provide a climate and atmosphere where my spouse, my children, and all the people I develop relationships with can express their feelings freely and fulfill their needs." During the Mitchell years we would meet halfway between Mitchell and Omaha (in Yankton, South Dakota) for a weekend of fun.

Moe's next move was to Newton, Iowa, to serve as President of one of the largest PCAs in the state. By this time, the agricultural economy was beginning to unravel and it wasn't long after that before I found myself as a former employee of the organization. I talked to Moe several times during my period of unemployment and he was always encouraging and supportive. (He did not offer me a job, though.) We ended up moving to Kansas City where I had several jobs before I finally found my dream job, working with credit unions all over the state of Missouri. In 2006 my wife and I both retired from our jobs and moved to St. Louis, Missouri, to be close to our grandchildren. We no longer see Moe and Mardi as often as we used to because travel is harder for us now, but we stay in touch.

I was packing my bags to fly to Atlanta, Georgia, for a national meeting of credit union execs early Monday morning when the phone rang one Sunday night about 10 PM. It was Moe. He was calling to tell me that his son, Jared, had been killed in an auto accident the previous week and the funeral had been the previous day. I had been unaware of it and was not there to support him in his time of need. Here is where I fell down on my taking the high road to personal accountability. I should have gone to Omaha, Nebraska, the following morning instead of to Atlanta, but I put my employer's needs in front of my friend's. I have never forgiven myself for that and never will. I did spend a good day with him a few days later. We cried and laughed and talked about Jared and about life and I felt like I might have said the right thing a couple of times that day…. but I still was not there at the time I should have been. Jared's death changed Moe and Mardi. They passed through the five stages of grief—denial, anger, bargaining, depression, and acceptance—very slowly and the process wore them down. There is a hole in their hearts that will never be filled.

My parents lost a son and I saw the difference it made in them for the rest of their lives. They were never the same. A light had gone out in their soul, and even though I presented them with three lovely grandchildren, the light never came back on as brightly as it had glowed before my brother's death. I am sure it is the same with Moe and Mardi.

I have known Moe for nearly fifty years and, in all that time, I have never known him to be anything other than totally committed to whatever he was giving his time to. If he was in a conversation, he was focused on that conversation. He gave himself totally to the Farm Credit System for all the years he worked there and, while we often discussed our perceived weaknesses in the organization that employed us, he was never critical of the organization's leadership. His reading consisted of farm publications, business periodicals, and books from which he thought he could learn things to make himself a better person. He was and is focused on becoming a better person every day. Moe has become very successful over the years and very much enjoys the comforts that he has acquired as the result of his efforts. I have known many people in my life who have achieved a high degree of economic well-being, some through their own efforts, and others through the good fortune to have been born well or married well, and others who won through good fortune (lotteries, etc.). I know few of them who did not let their position of wealth and power affect the way they treated others around them, including their family members, their communities, and their relationships. Moe has never changed from the hardworking, thoughtful, highly motivated leader that I first met on the very first day of his career. I am honored to be his friend and even more honored that he asked me to write some words for this book.